DWELLING PLACES

Phoenix·Poets

A SERIES EDITED BY ROBERT VON HALLBERG

DAVID FERRY

DWELLING PLACES

Poems and Translations

THE UNIVERSITY OF CHICAGO PRESS
Chicago and London

DAVID FERRY, Sophie Chantal Hart Professor of English at
Wellesley College, is the author of three previous books of poetry, *On
the Way to the Island*, *Strangers: A Book of Poems*, and *Gilgamesh: A New
Rendering in English Verse*. He is also the author of *The Limits of
Mortality*, a book about Wordsworth.

The University of Chicago Press, Chicago 60637
The University of Chicago Press, Ltd., London
© 1993 by The University of Chicago
All rights reserved. Published 1993
Printed in the United States of America
02 01 00 99 98 97 96 95 94 93   1 2 3 4 5

ISBN: 0-226-24478-4 (cloth)   0-226-24479-2 (paper)

Library of Congress Cataloging-in-Publication Data

Ferry, David.
    Dwelling places: poems and translations / David Ferry.
        p. cm. —(Phoenix poets)
    I. Title. II. Series.
    PS3556.E77D9 1993
    811'.54—dc20   92-31605
                                               CIP

For my family

—"Even unto this present hour we hunger, and thirst, and are naked, and are buffeted, and have no certain dwelling place."

—1 Corinthians 4:11

Contents

Acknowledgments

Grateful acknowledgment to the journals and other publications in which some of these poems have first appeared:

Agni "Autumn," "Horses," "In the Garden"

Arion: A Journal of the Humanities and the Classics, at Boston University (Third Series 1.1, Winter 1990) "Prayer to the Gods of the Night" (Also in *Lingering Over Words: Studies in Ancient/Near Eastern Literature in Honor of William L. Moran, Harvard Semitic Studies* (Atlanta: Scholars Press, 1990)

Boston Phoenix "Goodnight"

Eighteenth-Century Life "Civilization and Its Discontents"

Harvard Magazine (September–October 1992) "Harvesters Resting"

Justina: Homenaje a Justina Ruiz De Conde en su Ochenta Cumpleaños (Erie, Pa.: ALDEEU, 1992) "Unos Caballos"

The New Republic "A Young Woman"

Partisan Review (vol. 58, no. 4, 1991) "The Blind People" (translation of Charles Baudelaire poem)

Ploughshares "Nocturnal" (as "'Petrarchan'")

Poemata Humanistica Decem: Renaissance Latin Poems with English Translations (Somerville, Mass.: Firefly Press, The Houghton Library) "Of Violets"

Raritan "Abyss," "The Lesson," "At the Hospital," "Herbsttag," "The Guest Ellen at the Supper for Street People," "Mary in Old Age," "Mnemosyne," "Roman Elegy VIII," "Of Rhyme," "When We Were Children"

one

Strabo Reading Megasthenes

According to Megasthenes' own account
the wild man has no mouth with which to eat,

but only a breathing-orifice to breathe with.
He lives on the odor of fruits, and of flowers blooming,

or on the smell of faraway roasting meat.

Dives

The dogheaded wild man sleeps in the back alley,
behind the fence with bittersweet adorned,
in the corner of the garden over near
where the viburnum flowers or fails to flower,
depending on whether or not we water it.
Many times over again it has survived.
The leaves are homely, crudely rough-cut, with
a texture like sandpaper; an unluscious green,
virtuous in look, not really attractive;
like Kent in *Lear* plainspoken, a truth-teller,
impatient with comparison as with deceit.

The wild man sleeps in the maple-shaded alley
hidden behind the garden fence behind
the wooden garden seat weathering gray
in the corner of the garden over near
where the Orson Welles Movie Theater used to be,
from which in former days you faintly heard
the voices of the great dead stars still vying
in rich complaint, or else in exaltation
of meeting or farewell, in rituals
of wit o'ermastered, or in ecstasy
of woe beyond the experience of saints.

In the alley between the yard and the old theater
the wild man is, covered with leaves or clad
in the bark of our indigenous flourishing trees,
elaborately enscrolled and decorated
with the names of heavenly pity; there he sleeps
in the freedom of his distress among abandoned
containers of paint, eggshell and off-white tincts,
umbers both raw and burnt, vermilion, rose,
purples, and blues, and other hues and shades,
close by the tangled roll of wire screening,
under a scribbled hieroglyphic sign.

The Guest Ellen at the Supper
for Street People

The unclean spirits cry out in the body
or mind of the guest Ellen in a loud voice
torment me not, and in the fury of her unclean
hands beating the air in some kind of unending torment—
nobody witnessing could possibly know the event
that cast upon her the spell of this enchantment.

Almost all the guests are under some kind of enchantment:
of being poor day after day in the same body;
of being witness still to some obscene event;
of listening all the time to somebody's voice
whispering in the ear things divine or unclean,
in the quotidian of unending torment.

One has to keep thinking there was some source of torment,
something that happened someplace else, unclean.
One has to keep talking in a reasonable voice
about things done, say, by a father's body
to or upon the body of Ellen, in enchantment
helpless, still by the unforgotten event

enchanted, still in the old forgotten event
a prisoner of love, filthy Ellen in her torment,
guest Ellen in the dining hall in her body,
hands beating the air in her enchantment,
sitting alone, gabbling in her garbled voice
the narrative of the spirits of the unclean.

She is wholly the possessed one of the unclean.
Maybe the spirits came from the river. The enchantment
entered her, maybe, in the Northeast Kingdom. The torment,
a thing of the waters, gratuitous event,
came up out of the waters and entered her body
and lived in her in torment and cried out in her voice.

It speaks itself over and over again in her voice,
cursing maybe or not a familiar obscene event
or only the pure event of original enchantment
from the birth of the river waters, the pure unclean
rising from the source of things, in a figure of torment
seeking out Ellen, finding its home in her poor body.

Her body witness is, so also is her voice,
of torment coming from unknown event;
unclean is the nature and name of the enchantment.

Committee

Coldly the sun shone down on the moonlit scene.
Our committee stirred uneasily in its sleep.
Better not know too much too soon all about it.
The knees of grammar and syntax touched each other,
furtive in pleasure under the oaken table.

The river lay not moving under the light
of the shadowy earthly winter lunar scene.
*The ends of justice are determined in
the conditions of our sleep.* The spellbound scene
arranged itself in a traditional way,

transfixed and perfectly still. Unspoken agreements
spoke volumes on the bookshelves of the room.

Civilization and Its Discontents

Under the burin's meditative gaze,
caught in the cross-hatching and close-working
of the great engraving of the great painting
Fêtes vénitiennes, entangled in
the entrapment of the scription, as if in vines
entangled, or the entanglement of the veins,
it is Watteau himself, a naked soul,
suffering the humiliation and pain
of the company of fellow human beings,
dressed up as a country shepherd pretending to play
the bagpipe or musette for them to dance to,
looking over at what's-his-name, at Vleughels,
monstrously civilized great Turkey cock
here shown displaying all his gorgeous plumage
in grandiose dance, while all about in studied
mutual disposition others were,
and Venus was, presiding over the scene,
and over all this the great embroidered trees.

The Blind People

—Baudelaire

What is the difference between the unlimited
blackness they walk in this ridiculous
fashion through, and the eternal silence?
The sounds of the city, with all its laughter and music,
are a denial I walk through with my stupid
questions when I look at them. What are they
looking up at the sky for, with such blind
scrutinizing? Just think about them. How foolish,
and terrible, they look; weird; sleepwalkers;
puppets on a string, the divine light gone
forever from their eyes; and still they keep on
staring up at the sky; they never bow
their dreaming heads in noble meditation
over the pavements of the raucous city.

The Proselyte

A man the unclean spirits had gotten into
got into the parish hall on Tuesday night.

The unclean spirits poured out through his skin
in the form of filth and cried out in that form,

and cried out in the form of how he went
rapidly back and forth as if on many

errands to one person and another
or to nobody, up and down the parish hall,

little trips back and forward rapidly,
like a wasp or fly, hysterical with purpose,

battering himself against our difference.
There was authority in him as he went

carrying his message to one of us and another.
Who had condemned him to this filth and to

this unavailing rage? And the little voice
crying out something in the body's cage?

The voice was pitifully small, as if
from someplace else or time of childhood, say,

or country other, telling us something no one
in the parish hall could possibly understand,

rabbinical, as if of ancient learning
knowledgeable, and unintelligible,

a proselyte, the morphemes were uncouth.
His body was clad in the black of the unclean spirits.

And then he was gone away from the dining room,
a wasp trapped in a house, desperately trying,

flying from one room into another room,
how to get out of the place in which it was,

or else to carry the message to some place other.
He went to the phone on the wall of the hall outside

and said into the phone whatever it was he was saying,
and tore the phone out of the wall and talked to the wall,

telling it things in the tiny far-off doleful
insect crying voice in that other language.

And then he went to the outside door and said
to the outside door of the parish hall whatever

it was he said to us and the phone and the wall;
and then he was gone away into the night.

two

A Young Woman

That she, with such gifts given,
in the abundance and grace

of her youth and sweetness,
as if in a garden, walking,

in a summer of freshness
and of the wind lifting

and falling in a lavishing
of light and penultimate

shadow, that she should falter
at all through this phase,

pressing, with hand outstretched,
the surface of the future,

as one who is blind presses
the surface of darkness,

of corridor, or wall,
for any assurance at all,

may she be blessed
in this faltering forward.

Goodnight

Lying in bed and waiting to find out
whatever is going to happen: the window shade

making its slightest sound as the night wind,
outside, in the night, breathes quietly on it;

it is parental hovering over the infantile;
something like that; it is like being a baby,

and over the sleep of the baby there is a father,
or mother, breathing, hovering; the streetlight light

in the nighttime branches breathing quietly too;
altering; realtering; it is the body breathing;

the crib of knowing: something about what the day
will bring; and something about what the night will hold,

safely, at least for the rest of the night, I pray.

Nocturnal

It is always among sleepers we walk.
We walk in their dreams. None of us
knows what he is as he walks
in the dream of another. *Tell me my name*.
Your tongue is blurred, honeyed with error.
Your sleep's truth murmurs its secret.

Tell me your name. Out at the edge,
out in the cold, out in the cold
that came into the house in your clothes
the wind's hands hold onto nothing,
moaning, over the edge of the cliff
the wind babble unintelligible.

Abyss

—Baudelaire

Pascal's abyss was with him everywhere.
Everything is an abyss. Anything
that is done; that happens; is thought; is put into words.
I can't begin to tell you how many times
the fear in the sound of the wind has made my skin creep.

The deep; the long white empty beach stretching on
for ever; the silence; the desire of falling.
God has written out something on the face of the dark
in a hand absolutely sure of what it is doing.

I am afraid of sleep because I am afraid
of a hole empty with horror. I can see nothing
out of my window but infinity.

My acrophobic spirit is falling in love—
to be nowhere! —free of being, form, and name!

Name

I wish I could recall now the lines written across the surface of my dream.
They said Name investigated the possibility of its own
happiness muttering and frowning preoccupied so that it noticed
nobody else at all though somehow you could tell that it knew somebody
was standing there in the doorway looking in at it and watching
what it was doing rummaging in deskdrawers opening notebooks shutting
them up again writing down something or other on a scrap of paper
which would very soon be carelessly thrown away in a wastebasket and
go off in the trash somewhere out of the city burning stinking
        unrecoverable although not biodegradable

Of Rhyme

The task is the discovering of a rhyme
whose consequence is just though unforeknown
either in its completion having been
prepared for though in secret all the time

or in the way each step of the way brings in
to play with one another in the game
considerations hitherto unknown,
new differences discovering the same.

The discovering is an ordering in time
such that one seems to chance upon one's own
birth name strangely engraved upon a stone
in consequence of the completion of the rhyme.

Epigram

As with the skill of verses properly managed
the little river quietly makes its way
along the valley and through the local village
below the smiling hospitable house,
easily flowing over the shining stones,
trochee, and anapest, pyrrhic, and also spondee,
under the heartbeat easy governance
of long continued metrical discipline.

Its fields and woods in their good order are
a figure for the manners of that house:
disposed for intelligent pleasure, and for welcome.

Autumn

—Rilke

The autumn leaves are falling,
falling as if from far
heavenly groves whose leaves
are gesturing as they fall,
hands protesting their falling.

The earth is falling too,
falling through the night
among indifferent stars.

See, this hand is falling.
All of us are falling.
It is in everything.

(Yet there is One who holds
carefully in His hand
everything falling forever.)

Garden Dog

In the winter, out in the winter
sunlight, watched from the upstairs

window, by the binocular eye,
out in the winter light

the dog is wandering, sniffing
for enemies burrowed in Ireland

sometime in the nineteenth century.
What's in a dog's heart?

The terrier brown coat
touched into orange flame,

blue, purple, pink,
by the binocular gaze,

the brilliant monster is wandering,
smelling the winter air.

The wind is light. The light
is wandering, blown by the breezes.

What's in the way the sun shines down?
Sniffing the sticks and stones,

sniffing the dirt and dormant
unflourishing grass in the garden,

out in the winter light.

Horses

—for Tom Sleigh

It is true that, as he said, the horses,
when the lightning signaled something
along the horizon, acknowledged the signaling,

moving about in extraordinary beauty
of shifting and neighing, flicker of ear,
changings of pace, slidings, turnings,

the delicate legs finding out something
the ground could tell them, interpreting
the sky's statement of oncoming darkness.

The storm was doing whatever it does,
matrix of signaling, along the horizon.
In the valley the houses were brilliantly

clear, the storm's darkness was making
possible a perfect delineation,
the houses' edges brimming with light.

Unos Caballos

—Jorge Guillén

There are several horses grazing in the field,
motionless almost, untroubled as the grass

silently growing there in the light of the natural
morning before the beginning of anything human.

Docile in the confines of the pasture,
these hairy, unyoked, idle, quiet creatures

in vegetative peacefulness show no sign
of understanding. Their shadowed eyes and tranquil

ears know nothing of the vigil that they keep.
The serenity of heaven is realized

in their obliviousness of it, grazing there.

Roof

Four or five men on the high roof
of the apartment house I see from out my window,

angels or other beings from an element
other than ours but similar although

superior so bright and clear, perfected
in diminutive particular; angels

or little brilliant demons or simian
creatures with nose-and-mouth mask snouts

against the fumes of the material
a tiny glittering machine is putting down.

The fumes are visible and drift away,
like martyred souls made visible in the radiant air.

At the Hospital

As with the soft authority of wings
obscurely rustling, angels, we, or else
expressionless as policemen, in our clothes,
carefully unaccusing brought the word
of health and gladness as we passed along
the shining hospital corridor in the brilliant
frightening Sixties to the final place
where on her wretched bed my sister Betts
lay dying at the bottom of her room.

Above her head, on the television screen,
endlessly dying on the hotel floor
lay Bobby Kennedy as about him danced
the dance of consternation flittering out
along the echoing channels of the night.

A Morning Song

A bird cried out among the first things of the morning.
I dreamed about murders all night long.

It was the bird's cry that startled up the stone.
The stone changed color among the shadows as the sun came up.

Of Violets

—Politian

O beautiful violets, seeming to give such promise
of the fulfillment of love, the gift of her
whom I love, what is the nectar the tender winds
have scattered over your petals, making them fragrant?
What is the place of your birth? Was it under the care
of radiant Venus, there in the fields near the spring
of Acidalia? Was it under the care
of the god of love in the Idalian grove?

It must be that these are the same flowers
with which the Muses decorate their lyres
to play upon on the flowerbank of Permessus,
that these are the same flowers with which the maidens
Hora, Gratia, Aurora have adorned themselves
in the hour of the opening day. These must be the same
flowers that bloom in the violet beds of the garden
of the Hesperides, in the silent grove
the held breath of the wind possesses. These
violets are the springtime offering of Chloris;
the virtuous shades of the dead come back to play
among the grasses the violets intersperse.

Too happy violets, which that hand plucked
that wrenched me, miserable, from myself—
she held you, violets, to her lips, perhaps;
perhaps her lips and breath have breathed on you
the breath of her whom I love, the changing colors
of her breathing, making you blush and pale;
from the breath of her lips your fragrance is breathed upon you;
the sovereignty of her fragrance clings to you.

O most fortunate violets, who are
my life and my delight, the place of keeping,
the haven of my heart's longing, violets,
whom I touch and kiss in pain in thought of her,
these tears I shed nourish the fires of love
whose slow burning issues in these tears.
Be with me now forever, violets;
let neither the heat of summer nor winter's cold
deprive me of your solace, solace of pain;
stay with me now, perpetual in beauty,
O violets, O quietness of heart,
for I am in the wretchedness of love,

creature of sighs and weeping, because of my lady.

Levis Exsurgit Zephirus

—Goliardic

The wind stirs lightly as the sun's
warmth stirs in the new season's
moment when the earth shows everything
she has, her fragrance on everything.

The spring royally in his excitement
scatters the new season's commandment
everywhere, and the new leaves open,
the buds open, and begin to happen.

The winged and the fourfooted creatures
according to their several natures
find or build their nesting places;
each unknowingly rejoices.

Held apart from the season's pleasure
according to my separate nature
nevertheless I bless and praise
the new beginning of the new days,

seeing it all, hearing it all,
the leaf opening, the first bird call.

Herbsttag

—Rilke

Now is the right time, Lord. Summer is over.
Let the autumn shadows drift upon the sundials,
and let the wind stray loose over the fields.

Summer was abundant. May the last fruits be full
of its promise. Give them a last few summer days.
Bring everything into its completion, Lord,
the last sweetness final in the heavy wine.

Who has no house will never have one now;
who is alone will spend his days alone;
will wake to read some pages of a book;
will write long letters; wander unpeacefully
in the late streets, while the leaves stray down.

The Lesson

—from the Latin of Samuel Johnson

The stream still flows through the meadow grass,
as clear as it was when I used to go in swimming,
not good at it at all, while my father's voice
gently called out through the light of the shadowy glade,
trying to help me learn. The branches hung down low
over those waters made secret by their shadows.
My arms flailed in a childlike helpless way.

And now the sharp blade of the axe of time
has utterly cut away that tangle of shadows.
The naked waters are open to the sky now
and the stream still flows through the meadow grass.

In the Garden

The impatiens in the tub, beside the wooden bench
I'm sitting on, has leaves that are uniformly
a light green almost to the state of water,
different from the impatiens twenty feet away,
over by the birdbath. Are they a different
species or are the differences the result
of different conditions of light or earth?
The green of these leaves is almost an absence of green,
and the stalks look like rays of light under water.
The blossoms are pure white, with yellow centers.

I just this minute noticed that there are yellow
five-petaled flowers blooming in the little
patch of clover in the ground beside the tub.
These yellow flowers have centers of a paler
yellow growing out of a tender matrix
of green; and growing out of the same stalk
is a pod shaped like a little zucchini, or steeple,
pointed, tall by comparison with the flowers.
There is something springlike and free about the littleness,
oddness, and lightness of this combination of things,
observed here at the very tag end of summer,
in my good fortune.

                    Another little plant,
a weed I also don't know the name of,
with a white flower shaped like a deep cup,
and with blue-tipped sexual parts, lies in the grass,
the fallen maiden of some casual violence.
The whole plucked stalk is an event in time:
a number of blossoms one above the other,
but some blossoms more fully out than others,
in an intricately regular scale or series.
Of course, since the flower is plucked, it isn't really
an event in time, but only the record of an event.

Now there are a few leaves falling from the ash tree
in the steady mild wind. What's to come of all this
ill-informed staring at little flowers and
enigmatic misleading stalks and leaves?
It isn't autumn yet. There will be late autumn flowers.

When the wind started up suddenly just now,
when I was sitting in the garden reading Edward Thomas,
when I was looking at the back wall of our house,
soon to be different after the new porch is built,
when I had just had lunch with a friend who spoke
of how she used to be a lush and now
eats no meat, no sugar, and no dairy,
when my daughter in another part of the garden
was reading *The Mayor of Casterbridge*, and the branches
of the white fringe and the witch hazel shifted
suddenly, horizontally, and other branches

in the garden suddenly stirred and shifted, it was
as if these trees and bushes, the white ash, the sugar-
maple, the deutzia, the young unflowering pear tree,
had all suddenly had the same idea,
of motion and quiet sound and the changing light,
a subtle, brilliant, and a shadowy idea.

Roman Elegy VIII

—Goethe

When you tell me that you were unpopular as a child,
and that your mother spoke of you in a rueful

tone of voice, and that all this seemed to go on
for a very long time, the slow time that it took

for you to grow up, I believe you, and I enjoy
thinking about that odd, awkward child.

The grapevine flower, you know, is nothing much,
but the ripened fruit gives pleasure to men and gods.

When We Were Children

—"der Wilde Alexander" (fl. late 13th c.)

I remember how, at that time, in this meadow,
we used to run up and down, playing our games,
tag and games of that sort; and looked for wildflowers,
violets and such. A long time ago.
Now there are only these cows, bothered by flies,
only these cows, wandering about in the meadow.

I remember us sitting down in the field of flowers,
surrounded by flowers, and playing she loves me not,
she loves me; plucking the flower petals.
My memory of childhood is full of those flowers,
bright with the colors of garlands we wore in our dancing
and playing. So time went by among the wildflowers.

Look over there near those trees at the edge of the woods.
Right over there is where we used to find
blueberry bushes, blackberry bushes, wild strawberries.
We had to climb over rocks and old walls to get them.
One day a man called out to us: "Children, go home."
He had been watching from somewhere in the woods.

We used to feast on the berries we found in that place
till our hands and mouths were stained with the colors of all
the berries, the blackberries, strawberries, and the blueberries.
It was all fun to us, in the days of our childhood.
One day a man called out, in a doleful voice:
"Go home, children, go home, there are snakes in that place."

One day one of the children went into the grass
that grows high near the woods, among the bushes.
We heard him scream and cry out. He came back weeping.
"Our little horse is lying down and bleeding.
Our pony is lying down. Our pony is dying.
I saw a snake go crawling off in the grass."

Children, go home, before it gets too dark.
If you don't go home before the light has gone,
if you don't get home before the night has come,
listen to me, you will be lost in the dark,
listen to me, your joy will turn into sorrow.
Children, go home, before it gets to be dark.

There were five virgins lingered in a field.
The king went in with his bride and shut the doors.
The palace doors were shut against the virgins.
The virgins wept, left standing in the field.
The servants came and stripped the virgins naked.
The virgins wept, stripped naked, in the field.

three

Mnemosyne

—Hölderlin

I

Flowers, streams, hills, meadows, valleys—
everything beautiful praises the Lord,
in order to find out whether or not He is.

A wedding day is beautiful. Human arrangements,
the keeping of laws to shelter in, can break your heart.
He can change any or all of it just as He pleases.
Law is nothing He needs of what we know of it.

The hero desires to be in that condition,
where Truth *is* Being. The hero goes to the edge
and looks down over into whatever is there, or not,
in terror. God cannot do everything.
He cannot like the hero be in terror.

But everything is as it is, one way or another.
What does it all add up to, after all? Praise Him.

II

Peaceful scene: the sunlight on the lawns;
the shadowy branches over the dry paths;
the smoke blossoming from the chimney tops;
the lark song almost lost in the perfect sky;
the sheep and cattle feeding in the fields,
well-tended; the snow in the high meadows, flowering.

Value shining and flourishing everywhere.

Two people went this way, passing the cross
once placed there long ago for the pious dead,
two wanderers, one of them raging.

III

Under the fig tree my Achilles lies,
who died for me; and Ajax, near Scamander,
under the sound of the wind, at the grotto's mouth,
in a foreign country, far from Salamis.

Heroes have died, in one way or another.

Some were astonished in the bloodsoaked field,
in the experience of their fate, surrounded:
Patroclus in the armor of the king;
others, in torment and bewilderment,
by their own hand, compelled by heaven.

Things go all wrong when He takes hold of one of us.
But everything is as it is, one way or another.

four

Harvesters Resting

—after Millet

In the middle of the day, in the great shadow
of the grain stack, the harvesters
are resting and having their midday meal.

Boaz is approaching with a woman.
Meticulous as cattle in their attention
to the task of resting and feeding,
some of them seem not to have noticed.

Others regard her with the slow,
blind, thorough look that cattle have,
spellbound in the noontime heat.

Mary in Old Age

Yet—though dread Powers, that work in mystery, spin
Entanglings of the brain; though shadows stretch
O'er the chilled heart—reflect; far, far within,
Hers is a holy Being, freed from Sin.
She is not what she seems, a forlorn wretch,
But delegated Spirits comforts fetch
To Her from heights that Reason may not win.
      —Wordsworth

I

Mary's House

The bruised eyes and diffused radiant
face, anger *and* joy fused
in a question,
by what possible measure contained?

A skull's blood beating entirely
uninstructed against
whatever the world withheld against
the answer.

Nobody knew the answer.
The trees' dark bodies pressed up
against the house, like night by day,
how like a night by night.

II

Mary's Room at the Nursing Home

The room was like a room in a rented house
by the sea in the summer. The sun shone in

flatly and plainly, and sunlight and shadow
were disposed forthrightly and reasonably

across the surface of things, for instance on
the brown linoleum floor or on the simple

pine table painted a chalky green. There were decal
flowers on the headboard and footboard of the bed,

ignorant and cheerful about where they were.
As in a room to which one goes on vacation,

a rented place by the sea, there were very few
things one could call one's own, and these had a vivid

prominence: an open book on a table,
a vase of blue and white cornflowers, a brass clock.

Can Mary have been reading? Is the madness a hoax?
But the book on the table was a Harlequin romance

the attendant must just that moment have left off reading.
It was hot as anything. The curtains mimed

the letting in of air. Strangely girlish and wasted,
Mary lay on the little single bed

in a flowered summer dress, a naked Maja,
or like Olympia in the painting by Manet,

careless of everything, wanton, royal.

III

The Tower of Babel

She babbled barbarously and bravely,
with bravado and bravura,
a baby in a babushka, with a balalaika.

She was "a gate of God," a Babeler,
"Though babbling only to the Vale
of sunshine and of flowers,

bringing unto me
a tale of visionary hours."

IV

Of Others Who Were There

There was: the old lady in the nursing home
who kept coming up to me and standing much too close
to me, sniffing at my body or my soul
as if it was something deliciously stinking,

thrilling to her, or else a flowering bush,
nourishment for a ravenous questioning;
staring into my ear the way the child
in the comic routine long ago in the movies

stared silently into the coils of the ear
of the man sitting there next to the child,
trying to watch the movie on the screen,
driven wild inside by the child's relentless gaze:

as if the ear could speak its secrets back.

V

Mary Interpreter

Not a babble exactly, but words carefully chosen
to question the nature of her experience

in the bafflement of its own imprisoning nonsense.
Of the flowers I brought her on that summer day:

"When are you going to take them home and use them?"
and, "Yes, they were here, but I didn't see them,"

and, looking once again at the bouquet,
more closely, earnestly, and with suspicion:

"What is that? *Why did it go wrong?*"
Rocking a little in the rocking chair, she said,

"*I don't want to stay here. I want to stop it.*"
Was "here" the nursing home? Was it the chair?

The condition she was in? Her life? Life? The body?
Which of these things was it she wanted to stop?

Was she imprisoned in a world whose meanings
she was so familiar with that she needed to make

no translations at all, and no translation would be
anything but fatuous? Thus "Life" seems melodramatic,

too large and general to fit the case.
But "the chair" seems too small. And "the nursing home"

too obviously the right answer to be so.
In my reason and health I was outside this world,

translating her words with a too easy confidence.
But Mary was there, imprisoned in it, sovereign.

The scene changed in the way I experienced it.
It was as if I wasn't in the room

but in the empty lobby of some building.
Mary was in an open elevator,

old-fashioned, ornate, and beautiful.
The elevator kept moving up and down,

kept going down to the hell below—when I
leaned over and looked down then I could see

the suffering and also I could hear
sounds of the suffering too—then up again

to the hellish heaven above—peering up there
through the elevator shaft I saw and heard

the transcendental hilarious suffering there.
I heard voices as if there was singing or quarreling.

The Otis elevator never stopped at all.
Mary's body and spirit kept passing back and forth

before my eyes, vivid, free of the conditions
in terms of which her sympathetic friend,

standing in the deserted hallway, saw her
carried up and down in the elevator.

Over and over I saw her going past,
clinging to the bars, gesticulating,

frantic, confusingly like a figure of joy.
In the heat of the room on the summer day

Mary, standing now, began to unzip her dress,
with a slowness and persistence that suggested

an indecent purpose, a naked revelation
of body or soul, embarrassing to a visitor

there at the nursing home on a kind errand.
Perhaps she only wanted to unzip the dress

a little way, because of the summer heat.
But something about it seemed to refuse the suggestion.

There was a concentration and seriousness,
oblivious of the visitor and his thoughts,

as when she looked so earnestly at the bouquet.
We were in the same room and not in the same room.

I was in the same room. She was in a shirt of fire.
She was out on a plain crossed by steppe winds.

VI

Matthew 12:43–45

When the unclean spirit goes out of a person,
she walks for days and nights through the dry places,
looking for rest, and never finding any.
And then she says, "I will go home to my house,

from which I came." And so Mary goes there.
She finds it nicely swept and cleanly kept,
and pleasantly furnished, and garnished with flowers,
and empty, as if waiting for her to come home.

And then the unclean spirit goes and finds the other
unclean spirits. They come to her house together,
and get into the house, and live there, and it is worse
for her, much worse, than it had earlier been.

Prayer to the Gods of the Night

—Babylonian

The gates of the town are closed. The princes
have gone to sleep. The chatter of voices

has quieted down. Door bolts are fastened.
Not until morning will they be opened.

The gods of the place, and the goddess,
Ishtar, Sin, Adad, and Shamash,

have gone into the quiet of the sky,
making no judgments. Only

the voice of a lone wayfarer
calls out the name of Shamash or Ishtar.

Now house and field are entirely silent.
The night is veiled. A sleepless client

in the still night waits for the morning.
Great Shamash has gone into the sleeping

heaven; the father of the poor,
the judge, has gone into his chamber.

May the gods of the night come forth—the Hunter,
the Bow, the Wagon, the Yoke, the Viper,

Irra the valiant, the Goat, the Bison,
`Girra the shining, the Seven, the Dragon—

May the stars come forth in the high heaven.

Establish the truth in the ritual omen;
in the offered lamb establish the truth.

Envoi

Let these not be the black, imaginary
flowers of hell, nihilotropic,
turning their iron faces toward
no light but the light of the dead letter.

Notes

In the case of the translations I have simply cited under the title the name of the author or other source. I have not tried to differentiate between attempts at relatively close translation, freer rendering, and still freer adaptation.

I am greatly indebted to Rodney Dennis, Rodney Lister, William L. Moran, and Lawrence Rosenwald, among others, for translation suggestions and for active help in these matters. I have a general indebtedness also to Richard Bernheimer, *Wild Men in the Middle Ages*, New York, Octagon, 1979, and Timothy Husband, *The Wild Man: Medieval Myth and Symbolism*, New York, Metropolitan Museum of Art, 1980.

"Strabo Reading Megasthenes"—Strabo, *Geography*, 15.I.57, ed.
　　Leonard Jones, London, Loeb Classical Library, 1930.
"Civilization and Its Discontents"—see Sigmund Freud,
　　Civilization and Its Discontents, Chapter 2; Anne Claude
　　Phillipe, Comte de Caylus, "Vie de Watteau," *Vies des artistes du xviiiième siècle; Discours sur la peinture et la sculpture*, ed.
　　A. Fontaine, Paris, 1910. There is a translation in Edmond
　　and Jules de Goncourt, *French XVIII Century Painters*, ed.
　　and tr. Robin Ironside, London, Phaidon, 1948. The painting
　　is in the National Gallery of Scotland, Edinburgh. Nicolas
　　Vleughels (1668–1737), a painter, who later became director
　　of the French Academy in Rome. The engraving is by
　　Laurent Cars (1699–1771).

"The Blind People"—"Les Aveugles," *Les Fleurs du mal*.

"Abyss"—"Le Gouffre," *Les Fleurs du mal*.

"Autumn"—"Herbst," *Das Buch der Bilder*.

"Horses"—This poem is a response to reading Tom Sleigh's excellent poem "Three Horses," in *After One*, Boston, Houghton Mifflin, 1983.

"Unos Caballos"—*Cántico*.

"Of Violets"—"In Violas, A Venere Mea Dono Acceptas," *An Anthology of Neo-Latin Poetry*, ed. Fred J. Nichols, New Haven, Yale University Press, 1979. I am indebted to the prose translation in this volume, as well as for the Latin text.

"Levis Exsurgit Zephirus"—Peter Dronke, *The Medieval Lyric*, Cambridge, Cambridge University Press, 1977.

"Herbsttag"—*Das Buch der Bilder*.

"The Lesson"—Adapted from the Latin poem of Samuel Johnson, "Errat adhuc vitreus per prata virentia rivus," *Works*, Vol. 6, New Haven, Yale University Press, 1964, ed. E. L. McAdam, Jr., with George Milne. I am indebted to the prose translation in this volume.

"Roman Elegy VIII"—*Roman Elegies and Venetian Epigrams: A Bilingual Text*, ed. L. R. Lind, Wichita, University Press of Kansas, 1974.

"When We Were Children"—*German and Italian Lyrics of the Middle Ages*, ed. Frederick Goldin, New York, Anchor, 1973.

"Mnemosyne"—Based mainly on the first version of this poem by Hölderlin, with some use also of the third version. The original text of the first version is in Friedrich Hölderlin, *Sämtliche Werke*, Leipzig, 1926; the second in Richard Sieburth, ed., *Hymns and Fragments*, Princeton, Princeton University Press, 1984; and the third in Michael Hamburger, ed., *Poems and Fragments*, Ann Arbor, Michigan University Press, 1967. I am especially indebted here to Rodney Dennis and Lawrence Rosenwald.

"Harvesters Resting"—The title is the title of a painting by Millet in the Museum of Fine Arts, Boston. Originally Millet called it "Ruth and Boaz."

"Mary in Old Age" —The Wordsworth epigraph is from the "Miscellaneous Sonnets," III.36. Lines in "The Tower of Babel" have been adapted from Wordsworth, "To the Cuckoo."

"Prayer to the Gods of the Night"—Based on the literal translation from the Old Babylonian by William L. Moran.